ANTIGUA
AND BARBUDA

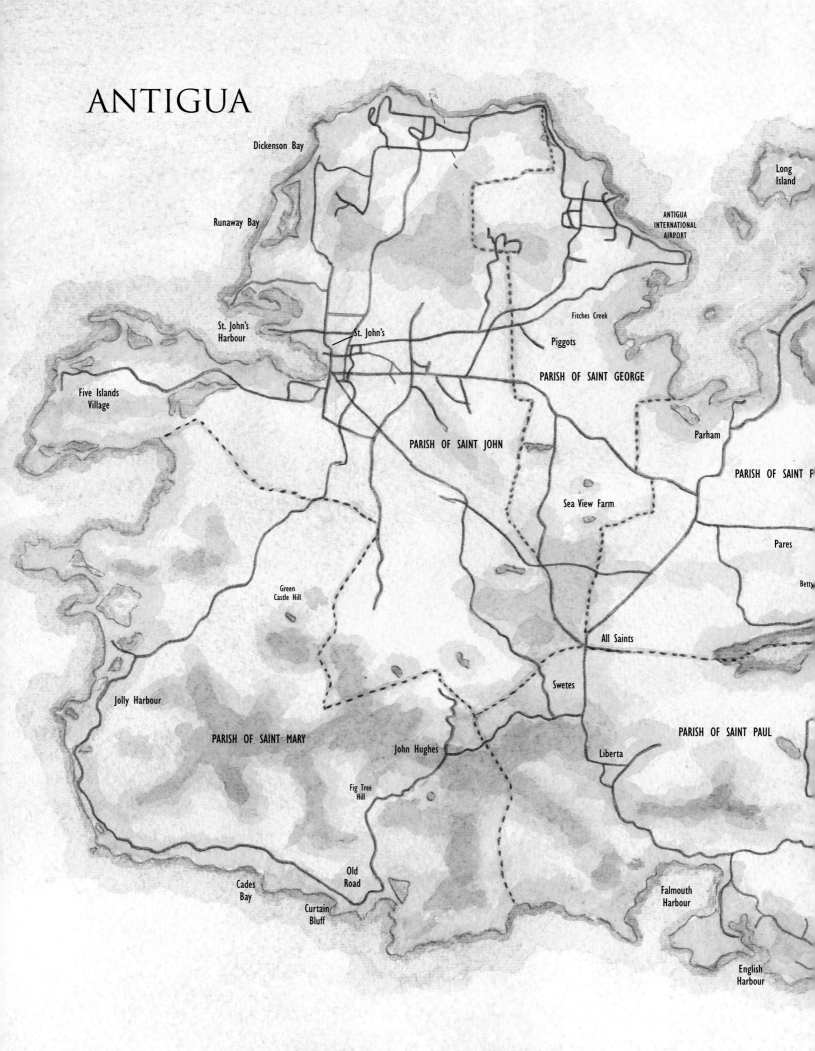

ANTIGUA

Dickenson Bay

Long Island

Runaway Bay

ANTIGUA INTERNATIONAL AIRPORT

St. John's Harbour

Fitches Creek

St. John's

Piggots

PARISH OF SAINT GEORGE

Five Islands Village

PARISH OF SAINT JOHN

Parham

PARISH OF SAINT P

Sea View Farm

Pares

Betty

Green Castle Hill

All Saints

Jolly Harbour

Swetes

PARISH OF SAINT MARY

John Hughes

PARISH OF SAINT PAUL

Liberta

Fig Tree Hill

Cades Bay

Old Road

Falmouth Harbour

Curtain Bluff

English Harbour

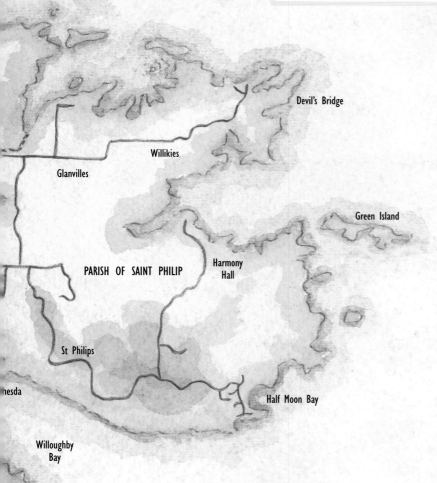

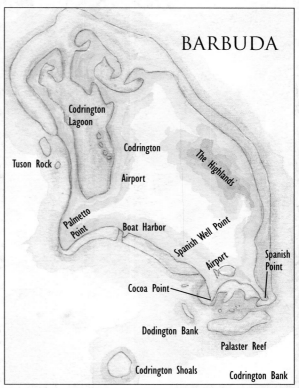

ANTIGUA
AND BARBUDA

A Photographic Journey

BARBUDA

Codrington Lagoon

Codrington

Tuson Rock

Airport

The Highlands

Palmetto Point

Boat Harbor

Spanish Well Point

Airport

Spanish Point

Cocoa Point

Dodington Bank

Palaster Reef

Codrington Shoals

Codrington Bank

Devil's Bridge

Willikies

Glanvilles

Green Island

PARISH OF SAINT PHILIP

Harmony Hall

St Philips

Half Moon Bay

nesda

Willoughby Bay

St. James Club

DANA JINKINS AND JILL BOBROW

WITH DESMOND NICHOLSON

PRODUCED BY CONCEPTS PUBLISHING, INC.

A BOAT INTERNATIONAL PUBLICATION

FOR CHRISTIAN

PRODUCED BY CONCEPTS PUBLISHING, INC.
Bridge Street Marketplace, Waitsfield, VT 05673
Tel. (802) 496-5580   Fax (802) 496-5581   E-mail concepts @madriver.com

A BOAT INTERNATIONAL PUBLICATION
IN ASSOCIATION WITH CONCEPTS PUBLISHING, INC.
5-7 Kingston Hill, Kingston-upon-Thames, Surrey KT2 7PW England
Tel. 44 (0) 181 547-2662   Fax 44 (0) 181 547-1201

Distributed by W.W. Norton & Company, Inc. in the U.S. and Canada
500 Fifth Avenue, New York, N.Y. 10110
ISBN   0-393-04784-9

Distributed by Edisea Ltd. in the rest of the world
ISBN   1-898524-75-0

Printed in Singapore by Star Standard Industries

GRAPHIC DESIGN AND LAYOUT   BONNIE ATWATER /ATWATER DESIGN
COPY EDITOR   JANET HUBBARD BROWN
MAPS   SARAH MELROSE

EDITOR'S NOTE: This book has been written in American English. When a word is used generically, we use the
American spelling. When part of a place name, i.e. English Harbour, we use the British spelling.

CONTENTS

(ABOVE) FERTILE FARMLAND NEAR BUCKLEYS IN THE PARISH OF ST. JOHN.

INTRODUCTION

Antigua and Barbuda are two small islands which comprise one country in the Eastern Caribbean. Formerly Associated States of Great Britain, they were granted independence in 1981. Antigua covers an area of 108 square miles and lies roughly in the middle of the Leeward Islands which form the most northerly group of the Lesser Antilles. It is a popular tourist destination with a rich history. Barbuda, 27 miles north of Antigua, with only 1600 inhabitants, is much less well-known than Antigua. However, with miles of beautiful beaches and turquoise shoal water, it has its own special charm.

Populated by Amerindians at the time Christopher Columbus arrived in 1493, Antigua and Barbuda did not have a European settlement until 1625 when the Earl of Carlisle claimed them to be under British protection. Evidence of British colonial influence can be spotted all over Antigua with sugar plantations scattered around the countryside and most significantly the large naval complex at English Harbour which dates back to the 17th century.

In addition to its interesting history, Antigua is particularly well-known as the yachting center of the Caribbean—you can cruise around Antigua and Barbuda for two weeks without stopping in the same anchorage twice.

When we decided to produce this book, we discovered that there is much more to Antigua and Barbuda than just the coastline. In exploring the interior, from dirt road to donkey path, we met many people and unearthed places not immediately obvious. This visual pastiche is both a photographic journey and a geographical tour that highlights places of interest parish by parish. Desmond Nicholson, a long-time resident of Antigua and an authority on these islands, has provided an historical essay as well as vintage photographs of Nelson's Dockyard at English Harbour.

Jill Bobrow

NELSON'S DOCKYARD

In Antigua's southeast corner lies a jewel of a harbor, completely enclosed by land and rugged hills. During the 18th and 19th centuries, when the sugar trade so economically important to Europe's warring nations was threatened, the admirals of England's Royal Navy brought their sailing ships in to English Harbour to be maintained. A dockyard in the Eastern Caribbean also gave the British freer movement in the colonial trade, thus creating substantially more profit.

Being a small harbor, the dockyard wasn't developed beyond the great sailing ship days until recently. The old naval yard and associated fortifications that sit atop Shirley Heights overlooking the harbor remain a uniquely unspoiled historic site.

The very first ship recorded at English Harbour was a yacht—a charter yacht in fact—called *Dover Castle* that belonged to His Majesty George III. She had been chartered by the king in 1671 from a Colonel Stroude for official use by the British governor of the Leeward Islands. The yacht was used "to chase ye pirates," along with the more common purpose of transporting the governor to the islands that were a part of his domain. The *Dover Castle* was recorded as having survived a hurricane while anchored in the harbor.

History has come full circle, for the harbor has become a haven to charter yachts, adding an important dimension to Antigua and Barbuda's growing tourist industry. Yachts call for supplies, repair and recreation at Falmouth and English Harbours, now restored and redeveloped to serve pleasure craft plying the islands of the Eastern Caribbean.

English Harbour has always been ideally sheltered for ships to make their

own repairs, and between July and October it provided a hurricane haven. Also, the water ran deep right up to the land, making the harbor suitable for careening—the hauling down of masts so that ships' bottoms come above water for cleaning and painting. This prevented warships from having to sail hundreds of miles north to the American colonies for dry-docking.

Development started about 1725. At first a few storehouses and a fort were constructed on the east side of the harbor, as well as a careening wharf. They were so successful that an additional yard was built on the opposite (west) side. A 50-foot hill surrounded by coral heads was blasted away and used as fill to cover the coral, thus creating a splendid expanse of flat ground for an extended naval yard. All this work was done, not by bulldozer, but by 120 African slaves "cheerfully lent by the planters" from surrounding sugar estates. A special act was passed in 1744 stating that slaves must work in the yard from sunrise until

(PAGE 2) THE COPPER AND LUMBER STORE LOCATED IN THE DOCKYARD, ORIGINALLY BUILT IN 1789 AS A WAREHOUSE FOR MATERIALS USED FOR REPAIRING SHIPS' HULLS, IS NOW A CHARMING HOTEL.

. . . . .

(ABOVE) IN 1955 ENGLISH HARBOUR AND THE DOCKYARD WAS A MUCH QUIETER PLACE THAN TODAY.

. . . . .

(LEFT) CAREENING A BOAT TO SCRAPE AND PAINT THE BOTTOM WAS PRACTICED IN THE 1950S. TODAY— WHILE CAREENING IS STILL VIABLE— YACHTS ARE MORE LIKELY TO BE HAULED OUT OF THE WATER WITH A TRAVELIFT.

noon, minus an hour for breakfast. After a two-hour rest, they had to work until sunset. This wasn't an improvement over plantation work, as conditions there could be just as brutal. To this day, the people who built the dockyard have never been acknowledged.

By 1733 a water catchment with cisterns had been built by the planters to encourage naval ships to base at English Harbour. Visitor's can see the sailors' graffiti on its walls dating from 1739 to 1751. One can imagine these mariners, waiting for their barrels to fill, carving their names like schoolboys for us, an undreamed of generation, to wonder about in the far distant future.

WARS & WORKERS

English Harbour played an important part in the Seven Years' War that lasted from 1756 until 1763. Warships raided the Spanish Main and often limped back into the dockyard—known as the Antigua Navy Yard—for much-needed

(ABOVE) A VIEW OF YACHTS AT THE DOCKYARD FROM CLARENCE HOUSE ACROSS THE BAY.

· · · · ·

repairs. During the American Revolution there were about 210 workers in the yard, of which 70 percent were of African origin. "The King's Negroes" were artificer slaves owned by the Royal Navy and sometimes by leading planters of the island. These black artificers' skills were deemed so important that they were given their own servants, who were considered apprentices in their given trade. In 1780 19 black shipwrights and twenty black caulkers, for example, labored in the yard, as well as tradesmen who were perhaps paid a few cents a day. Slave names were often satirical or fanciful: Caesar, Samson, Monkey, Ben Bowsprit, Tom Bowline, Tom Tackle or Jack Ratline. They lived in a row of huts within the dockyard wall.

Resistance to work was often demonstrated; for example, Alexander, an apprenticed sailmaker, was sold in 1797, as he was "unmanageable." He was described as vicious and ungovernable and addicted to thieving, wounding and suicide. Workers' holidays were rare as there were only four annual holidays: the King's Birthday, Coronation Day, Restoration of the Monarchy Day (29 May) and Guy Fawkes Day (5 November). Sometimes after especially hard work a gang would be given a gallon of rum to drown their sorrows. The moral state of the dockyard was "deplorably wicked." According to sources of the time, the Sabbath was unknown; the yard bell rang on Sundays for natives, black and white, to work when ships of war anchored; immorality of the worst description was perpetrated. Methodist ministers, however, preached once a fortnight on weekday evenings. English Harbour was the "grave of Englishmen." There was no shade, too much drink and too many women: "These temporary wives not only diseased and debilitated the men, but procured them rum in exchange for provisions, bedding and clothes."

THE NELSON ERA

The history of English Harbour includes many famous people and visitors. Admiral Rodney came to English Harbor in 1762 to improve the efficiency of the yard, causing "officials to shake in their shoes." In 1784 Captain Horatio Nelson, age 26, and in command of the 28-gun frigate *Boreas* arrived. He was determined, even against Sir Thomas Shirley's orders, to enforce the Navigation Act, which stated that British ships were only to carry cargoes between British colonies. The Americans, now that they were independent, were considered "foreign." Needless to say, Nelson was extremely unpopular with the St. John's merchants for prohibiting trade with the ex-colonial Americans. There was a time when he would have been arrested and sued if he had stepped ashore.

At English Harbour, Nelson complained of the mosquitoes that "pinched him woefully." He usually started his day by having six pails of saltwater poured over his head and drinking a quart of goat's milk. In 1787, finding himself Senior Captain of the Station, Nelson became the Commander-in-Chief for six months before he sailed home. He took with him a barrel of rum in which to preserve his body should he die, as he was suffering from chronic tropical illness.

RISE & FALL

The heyday of the yard climaxed during the Napoleonic Wars when five officers and 327 workers were employed. In 1815, after the termination of a series

(ABOVE) BUILT IN 1855 AS A RESI-
DENCE FOR THE NAVAL OFFICER
AND THE STOREKEEPER IN CHARGE
OF THE DOCKYARD, THIS BUILDING
NOW HOUSES THE MUSEUM.

· · · · ·

(RIGHT) A LIKENESS OF THE FAMOUS
BRITISH ADMIRAL, LORD NELSON,
WHO WAS STATIONED IN THE
LEEWARD ISLANDS BETWEEN
1784 AND 1787.

(ABOVE) THE SAIL LOFT DEPICTED IN D.V. NICHOLSON'S 1950 PHOTOGRAPH PRESENTS
A PEACEFUL SCENE VOID OF COMPUTERS AND HIGH-TECH MACHINES.

. . . . .

(RIGHT) THESE PILLARS ARE THE REMAINS OF THE SAIL LOFT BUILT 200 YEARS AGO.
LONGBOATS ENTERED THE CHANNEL BETWEEN THE PILLARS UNDER THE LOFT AND PASSED
THEIR SAILS UP THROUGH A HATCH IN THE FLOOR.

of wars that had lasted well over a century, the workforce in the dockyard at English Harbour began to be reduced and gradually the harbor lost its importance. It continued to be maintained for another three-quarters of a century, even though, due to the Industrial Revolution, ships became too large for the harbor. The harbor was used as a coal station for small steamers, some of which belonged to the Royal Mail Packet Company. Later, when the only people in the yard were caretakers, warships of the Victorian Royal Navy entered the harbor and conducted their own self-refits. Finally, in 1889, HMS *Canada* was sent to close down the Antigua Navy Yard. By 1906 the Admiralty had finally handed over the dismantled dockyard to the Antiguan Colonial Government.

AN EMPIRE MEMORIAL

The old dockyard fell into disrepair, left to the mercy of earthquakes, hurricanes and entwining tropical vegetation. It became ghostlike, replete with cobwebs, banging shutters and sagging walls; bats flew around, and goats,

lizards, mice and mongoose were the only inhabitants. Then, Sir Reginald St. Johnston, governor of the Leeward Islands, took pity and realized it should not be allowed to deteriorate any further. In 1931 he established the Dockyard and Shirley Heights Restoration Fund to preserve the English Harbor area as an "Empire Memorial." A guidebook was published and the Officers' Quarters were restored by Sun Life Insurance of Canada.

FROM RUIN TO LIVING MONUMENT

Unfortunately, little was accomplished until Sir Kenneth Blackburne became governor in 1957. He saw a small ray of hope among the despairing hurricane refugees in the Officers' Quarters, for he had noticed a beautiful schooner, the *Mollihawk*, lying alongside one of the wharves. It was the first charter yacht of the eastern Caribbean and had already started taking cruises down island.

Blackburne thought the old buildings should be used again, this time by sailing ships and yachts rather than by military vessels. He also thought, why shouldn't the dockyard become a memorial to the great deeds of the Royal Navy, and furthermore, why not turn it into a tourist resort?

The Friends of English Harbour was created the following year, and eventually the dockyard was renamed "Nelson's Dockyard." A repair fund was started in London and in 1955, Lady Churchill hosted a luncheon at No. 10 Downing Street to support the project. The dockyard was gradually restored, so that in 1961, on Prince Charles' birthday, the yard was reopened by the Governor-General of the West Indies Federation with the theme, "From Ruin to Living Monument."

No repair facilities existed at the dockyard for the growing charter yacht fleet, so self-refits occurred on sailing vessels visiting English Harbour (for the third time in its long history). Yachts created much-needed employment and opportunities for self-employment for local residents. The timing was perfect as the island was in the midst of union strikes occurring around the dwindling sugar industry. Private enterprise around the yacht trade increased gradually. In the 1960s the first yacht yard was built at St. Helena, on the site of the first Antigua Navy Yard. A new industry for Antigua was born.

Nelson's Dockyard National Park was created in 1984 to preserve the area's history, and to provide a springboard for generating jobs and revenue for the people. Several years later, the Government announced an 11 million Eastern Caribbean dollar-development program provided by the Canadian International Development Agency to make the park into a world-class tourist attraction.

(TOP) THE DOCKYARD HAS UNDERGONE MAJOR RENOVATIONS.

(ABOVE) IN 1948, PRIOR TO RENOVATION, THIS WAS ALL THAT REMAINED OF THE CORDAGE AND CANVAS STORE.

(LEFT) IN FEBRUARY OF 1966, QUEEN ELIZABETH MADE A VISIT TO THE ISLANDS AND PLANTED A COMMEMORATIVE TREE IN ANTIGUA.

In this photo taken in 1954, a woman repairs sails in the shade. Beyond her to
the left is the building which now houses Nicholson's Yacht Sales, Lord Jim's
Locker and the liquor store, Crab Hole Too.

· · · · ·

A VIEW OF THE DOCKYARD IN 1954, AND THE FAMOUS CAPSTANS WHICH
WERE USED TO CAREEN THE BOATS.

. . . . .

(TOP LEFT) ADMIRAL'S INN—THIS CHARMING HISTORIC HOTEL AND
RESTAURANT IS EXTREMELY POPULAR WITH THE CRUISING CROWD.

(TOP RIGHT) THE BACK SIDE OF THE COPPER AND LUMBER HOTEL SHOWS HOW THE
ORIGINAL ARCHITECTURAL DETAIL HAS BEEN MAINTAINED THROUGHOUT THE RESTORATION PROCESS.

(BOTTOM LEFT) THE GALLEY BOUTIQUE IN THE CENTER OF THE DOCKYARD IS REPLETE WITH
CLOTHING AND GIFTS, FROM DESIGNER LABELS TO ANTIGUAN-MADE PRODUCTS.

(BOTTOM RIGHT) THE DOCKYARD "SHOPPING MALL."

· · · · ·

THE DOCKYARD IN 1989 LOOKS MUCH THE SAME AS IT DID IN 1954, NOW RENOVATED
AND FULLY OPERATIONAL.

· · · · ·

(MAIN PHOTO) A VIEW OF YACHTS
ANCHORED IN FREEMAN BAY FROM FORT
BERKELEY, WHICH IS LOCATED ON THE
PENINSULA THAT FORMS THE WEST
ENTRANCE TO ENGLISH HARBOUR.
THE FORT WAS STARTED IN 1704, AND
WAS LATER EXTENDED IN THE 1740S WHEN
MEMBERS OF THE BRITISH NAVY WERE
ENCAMPED AT THE DOCKYARD.

. . . . .

(BELOW) A CENTURY PLANT IN BLOOM.

THE PARISH OF
*S*T. PAUL

The parish of St. Paul represents the true hub of yachting activity in Antigua because of its six marinas and fine anchorages. In English Harbour there is Nelson's Dockyard as well as the full-service marina at Antigua Slipway.

At Falmouth Harbour is the Antigua Yacht Club Marina, centrally situated among shops, boutiques and restaurants. Falmouth Harbour Marina, a relatively new facility, is located between Falmouth Port Authority and the Pumps and Power Dinghy Dock. Situated at the northwest side of the harbor is the charming and popular Catamaran Hotel and Marina.

The St. Paul parish has a large concentration of foreign residents and a host of transient yacht crews. New shops and businesses that cater to them are opening every day. Restaurants range from local shacks selling *Rasta* dishes and *roti* to European-style establishments creating Italian wood-fired pizza and French *haute cuisine*. At night steel drums, calypso, reggae and hip hop can be heard at many of the eateries, bars and hotels.

The main road out of English Harbour leads to Cobb's Cross where you follow the road to the lovely St. James Club Hotel and Marina on Mamora Bay, passing the University of Health Science (Antigua's medical school) and the famous, but not well-frequented, Bat's Cave. Following the western coast of Willoughby Bay through pleasant rolling scenery, you reach the village of Bethesda where in 1813 the first school was opened to slaves. In 1834, after the emancipation of the slaves, the town grew up around the schoolhouse. From Bethesda the road leads around the eastern side of Potswork Dam Reservoir before heading back to St. John.

(PAGE 20) SUNSET VIEW FROM SHIRLEY HEIGHTS.

. . . . .

(ABOVE) THREE PRIMARY SCHOOLS SERVE THE
CHILDREN OF FALMOUTH HARBOUR: THE TWO PUBLIC
SCHOOLS AND AN ALTERNATIVE PRIVATE SCHOOL.

(RIGHT) FISHING BOATS MOORED OFF THE
VILLAGE OF PATTERSONS, FALMOUTH HARBOUR.

(ABOVE) VIEW OF FALMOUTH BAY FROM PATTERSONS.

· · · · ·

(RIGHT) OUR LADY OF PERPETUAL HELP, "TYRELL'S CHURCH" IN SWETES.

(MAIN PHOTO) AERIAL VIEW OF CAPE SHIRLEY WITH
INDIAN CREEK AND MAMORA BAY IN THE DISTANCE.
· · · · ·

(ABOVE) THE "PILLARS OF HERCULES" AT THE FOOT
OF CHARLOTTE PENINSULA. BEHIND THESE FAMED
PILLARS LIE THE RUINS OF THE UPPER AND LOWER
FORT CHARLOTTE (C. 1700-1830), NAMED AFTER
QUEEN CHARLOTTE, WIFE OF KING GEORGE III.

(ABOVE) FISHING BOAT ANCHORED IN FRONT OF THE CATAMARAN HOTEL.

· · · · ·

(OPPOSITE) SEVERAL HISTORIC BUILDINGS COMPRISE A MUSEUM IN ENGLISH
HARBOUR TOWN THAT SHOW HOW ANTIGUANS ONCE LIVED. THE EARLIEST
BUILDINGS WERE MADE OF WADDLE AND DAUB, WHICH ARE WOVEN STICKS
PLASTERED WITH MUD THEN ROOFED WITH CANE TRASH.

(MAIN PHOTO) ENGLISH HARBOUR AND FALMOUTH
HARBOUR FROM SHIRLEY HEIGHTS.

. . . . .

(ABOVE) THE LIGHT FIELD TRAIN building AT FORT SHIRLEY
DATES BACK TO 1813. FORT SHIRLEY WAS ONCE A LARGE
BRITISH MILITARY COMPLEX. CONSTRUCTION BEGAN IN THE
1780S AND CONTINUED INTO THE 1820S. IT WAS LAST USED BY
THE BRITISH IN 1854.

(BELOW) THE MAIN GUARDHOUSE AT FORT SHIRLEY.

(ABOVE) SUPERYACHTS DOCKED AT THE PRESTIGIOUS ST. JAMES CLUB DURING
THE NICHOLSON CHARTER SHOW, 1998.

· · · · ·

(RIGHT) THE ST. JAMES CLUB IS A LUXURY RESORT THAT OCCUPIES A BEAUTIFULLY
LANDSCAPED PENINSULA. HOTEL ROOMS AND VILLAS OVERLOOK EITHER
THE BAY OR THE OCEAN.

THE PARISH OF
St. JOHN

The parish of St. John cuts a swath through central and northwestern Antigua. St. John is the capital of Antigua and the only town of any size on the island. Initially laid out around the head of a large shallow harbor in the early 18th century, it has only blossomed in the last 25 years or so with the advent of cruise ship trade. "Town," which houses about one-third of the population of Antigua, is crowded and bustling with activity. Vehicles edging along the one-way streets can create traffic jams. Walking is the preferable method for viewing the fresh produce market and checking out the street stalls proffering everything from colorful paintings to beaded necklaces, hot sauce and shampoo. The most elegant boutiques are located around Redcliffe Quay and Heritage Quay, where you'll find the largest complex of duty-free shops. Several quaint corners with charming old wooden or stone buildings converted into shops and restaurants can be seen in other areas of town. The Museum of Antigua and Barbuda houses curiosities such as Arawak artifacts, archival papers and even a cricket bat! Another landmark is the Cathedral of St. John the Divine. The Anglican church, built in 1847, was constructed of cement-washed stone and has a pine interior.

Outside of town is an area known as Five Islands that has five rocky islets off the southern part of the bay. Traveling further north and west, Deep Bay offers secure protection for cruising yachts; for the landlubber, Runaway and Dickenson Bays are the main tourist destinations with their island-beautiful beaches, fine hotels, condominiums, villas and guest houses. Inland is the 18-hole golf course at Cedar Valley Golf Club.

PAGE 34: HEMINGWAY'S RESTAURANT IS A DELIGHTFUL LUNCHEON SPOT WITH A BIRD'S EYE VIEW OF ST. JOHN'S FROM THE WRAPAROUND UPPER DECK.

. . . . .

(OPPOSITE, TOP) A COLORFUL
ADVERTISEMENT FOR CARIB BEER
IS DISPLAYED ON THE SIDE OF A
BUILDING.

(OPPOSITE, BOTTOM LEFT) A LITTLE
GIRL IS PROUD TO SHOW OFF HER
PRETTY OUTFIT AND TOOTHY SMILE.

(OPPOSITE, BOTTOM RIGHT) ONE OF
THE MANY TABLESIDE "SHOPS" THAT
LINE THE SIDEWALKS OF ST. JOHN'S.
THEY OFFER A VARIETY OF GOODS,
FROM PEANUTS TO TOMATOES TO
COMBS.

. . . . .

(TOP, LEFT AND RIGHT) . . . . JUST
HANGIN' OUT, WATCHING THE
WORLD GO BY.

(BOTTOM, LEFT) A HAT VENDOR
HOPING THE ANTIGUAN SUN IS TOO
MUCH FOR THE PASSING TOURIST.

(ABOVE) OLD BUILDINGS PAINTED WITH BRIGHT COLORS AND CONVERTED INTO
SHOPS AND BOUTIQUES ADD TO THE CHARM OF ST. JOHN'S.

· · · · ·

(LEFT) A PAINTED MURAL ENHANCES THE FOUNDATION OF THIS COLORFUL BAR.

(ABOVE) FRANK'S PHOTO STUDIO ON MARKET STREET SURPRISINGLY
DOES NOT HAVE PHOTOS, BUT MINIATURE PAINTINGS OF FISH, ANIMALS
AND LANDSCAPES INSTEAD.

(LEFT) FRANCIS WALTER'S PAINTINGS COME DECORATIVELY FRAMED,
GLASS INCLUDED.

. . . . .

(RIGHT) A WOMAN SELLING HERBS

(PAGES 42-43) THE MARKET IS A BUSTLING PLACE, WITH EVERYONE
COMPETING TO SELL ROOT VEGETABLES, GREENS AND FRUITS. EVEN THOUGH
ANTIGUA IS NOT AS LUSH AS SOME OF THE CARIBBEAN ISLANDS, THERE IS STILL
A HEALTHY AMOUNT OF PRODUCE GROWN.

· · · · ·

(TOP) FISHING BOATS READYING THEIR CATCH FOR MARKET.

. . . . .

(BOTTOM, LEFT) LADIES AT THE FISH MARKET.

(BOTTOM, RIGHT) FRESH PARROT FISH.

(ABOVE) CRUISE SHIPS COME REGULARLY TO ST. JOHN'S WHERE HORDES OF TOURISTS DESCEND
TO SHOP AND JOIN BUS TOURS OF THE ISLAND.

· · · · ·

(TOP) TYPICAL COMMERCIAL STREET IN ST. JOHN'S.

(BOTTOM, RIGHT AND FAR RIGHT) UPSCALE SHOPS AND RESTAURANTS LINE THE WALKING STREET OF HERITAGE CAY WHERE SEVERAL CRUISE SHIPS CAN DOCK AT THE SAME TIME.

. . . . .

(OPPOSITE, TOP) THE BASE BOUTIQUE SELLS A LINE OF CLOTHES DESIGNED AND MADE IN ANTIGUA.

(OPPOSITE, BOTTOM) CARIBBEAN-STYLE VILLAGE HOUSE CONVERTED INTO A CHARMING SHOP.

(PAGES 48-49) CARNIVAL IN ANTIGUA TAKES PLACE THE LAST WEEK OF JULY. IT IS AN EXUBERANT FESTIVAL OF MUSIC, DANCE AND CAMARADERIE. ELABORATE COSTUMES ARE ARTISTICALLY CONCEIVED AND THE MUSIC IS A WONDERFUL MIX OF STEEL BAND AND CALYPSO. FOOD, DRINK AND PARTIES ARE PART OF THE FUN. IT IS A TIME OF HIGH SPIRITS THAT SHOULD NOT BE MISSED.

(PHOTOS THIS PAGE TOP LEFT AND RIGHT BY JENNIFER MERANTO; THIS PAGE BOTTOM, AND OPPOSITE PAGE, BY ALEXIS ANDREWS)

. . . . .

(PAGES 50-51) ST. JOHN'S CATHEDRAL, CONSECRATED IN 1848, WAS BUILT OF FREESTONE WITH AN INTERIOR OF PITCH PINE. PREVIOUSLY TWO ANGLICAN CHURCHES HAD STOOD ON THE SITE, THE FIRST AS EARLY AS 1681, AND THE SECOND IN 1720. DOMINATED BY TWIN TOWERS, THE ARCHITECTURE HAS A DISTINCT BAROQUE FEEL TO IT. THE SCULPTURES OF ST. JOHN THE DIVINE AND ST. JOHN THE BAPTIST SIT ATOP THE GATE.

· · · · ·

(TOP, LEFT) SMALL SHOP SELLING LOCALLY MADE CLOTHING.

(TOP, MIDDLE) WATER SPORTS FACILITIES AT
HALCYON COVE HOTEL.

(ABOVE) SIBONEY BEACH CLUB ON DICKENSON BAY IS A
LOVELY PLACE FROM WHICH TO VIEW THE SUNSET.

. . . . .

(MAIN PHOTO) SANDALS RESORT ON DICKENSON BAY.

(ABOVE) A VIEW OF TRAFALGER BEACH AND PILLAR
ROCK BAY, WITH SALT POND ON THE RIGHT.
(RIGHT) VIEW AS SEEN FROM GOAT HILL

. . . . .

(OPPOSITE, TOP) FORT BARRINGTON STANDS ON
THE NORTH SIDE OF DEEP BAY WITH
COMMANDING VIEWS ALL AROUND. THE FORT
WAS BUILT AS A BATTERY AND OBSERVATION
POST DURING ADMIRAL NELSON'S ERA.
(OPPOSITE, BOTTOM) VIEW OF HOG JOHN BAY
FROM FORT BARRINGTON.

THE PARISH OF
St. MARY

Encompassing the southwestern part of Antigua, Saint Mary's is notable for steep-sided hills, scenic views along drivable coastline, rural villages and a bit of rainforest. Past the town of St. John's on All Saint's Road, a picturesque route starts from where the road divides—the right hand fork running southward takes you through the villages of Buckleys, Swetes and John Hughes, skirting a green valley with dams and reservoirs. At Fig Tree Hill, where the road descends to the Old Road, large mango trees and fragrant lemon and banana groves line the way. Flamboyant trees are ablaze with firey orange-red blossoms, and kapok trees drip with cotton-like fluff balls.

At the head of Old Road is Carlisle Bay. On the headland to the west is the well-established Curtain Bluff Hotel. A two-mile-long reef lies up to one-and-a-half miles between the hotel and Pelican Island—the outer portion is called Cades Reef and the inner section is known as Middle Reef. This area is perfect for snorkeling and windsurfing.

Going north from the Cades Bay region, you see fields of pineapples under cultivation at the base of the Sherkeley Mountains. Antigua is not a very mountainous island; the highest summit, Boggy Peak (1,300 feet) is here. Back on Old Road and heading west is the new development of Jolly Harbour. With over seven miles of dredged waterfront, it is a large complex that includes a full-service marina, condominiums, hotel, restaurants and shops. Beyond Jolly Harbour, a country road leads to the surprising bucolic scenery of cow pastures and hills dotted with the random remains of old sugar mills. Eventually you will find yourself back in St. John's.

(PAGE 56) BOY ON EARLY MORNING RIDE AT BOLANS.

. . . . .

(ABOVE) A GUIDED HIKE DOWN A NATURE TRAIL NEAR
SIGNAL HILL IN WALLINGS FOREST.

(RIGHT) A COW EATING A MANGO.

. . . . .

(OPPOSITE) LUSH RAINFOREST VEGETATION ON
FIG TREE DRIVE.

(ABOVE) Fig Tree Drive is filled with banana groves,
palms and mango trees.

. . . . .

(OPPOSITE, TOP) A small shop that sells local products such as
guava jam and sour sop drinks.

(OPPOSITE BOTTOM, RIGHT) Ripe tamarinds and pineapples.

(OPPOSITE BOTTOM, FAR RIGHT) A lizard basks in the sun.

(ABOVE) WALLINGS RESERVOIR, STARTED IN 1890 AND FINISHED IN 1900, WAS DESIGNED TO HOLD 13 MILLION GALLONS OF WATER. HOWEVER, AFTER MANY DROUGHTS, IT IS INADEQUATE FOR SUPPLYING WATER TO SURROUNDING VILLAGES.

(BOTTOM, RIGHT) THE SPILLWAY OF THE DAM IS AN EXAMPLE OF VICTORIAN INDUSTRIAL ARCHITECTURE.

. . . . .

(OPPOSITE) PRIOR TO SYNTHETIC MATERIALS, THE FLUFFY COTTONY BALLS FROM THE KAPOK TREE WERE PUT IN THE FABRIC OF LIFE JACKETS FOR FLOTATION PURPOSES.

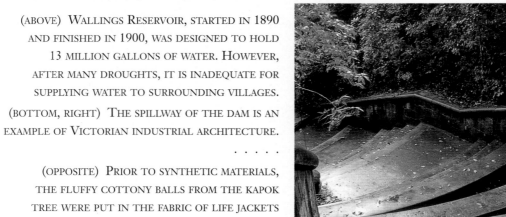

(RIGHT) BAOBAB TREES ARE RARE (THERE ARE ONLY THREE OF THEM ON THE ISLAND). THEIR LEAVES HAVE BEEN USED FOR FOOD AND MEDICINE, AND THEIR BARK FOR PAPER, CLOTH AND ROPE.

(MIDDLE) THE NATURE OF THINGS IS A SHELL SHOP IN URLINGS.

(BOTTOM) O.J.'S RESTAURANT AT CRAB HILL SPECIALIZES IN FRESH LOCAL DISHES AND GREAT ATMOSPHERE.

(ABOVE) PALM TREES AT GOAT HEAD.

· · · · ·

(MAIN PHOTO AND ABOVE) THE GREEN
CASTLE HILL AREA IS INTERESTING FOR ITS
UNIQUE LANDSCAPE OF ROLLING HILLS AND
VERDANT PEAKS.

· · · · ·

(MAIN PHOTO) JOLLY HARBOUR IS A LARGE NEW
MARINA AND CONDOMINIUM DEVELOPMENT WITH OVER
SEVEN MILES OF DREDGED WATERFRONT. IN ADDITION TO THE
SERVICES AND MAN-MADE FACILITIES, THE BEACH IS SUPERB.
. . . . .

(BELOW) MANY OF THE VILLAS HAVE THEIR OWN
PRIVATE DOCKS.

(PAGES 70-71) HUGH PIGGOTT HAS
DEVELOPED ORANGE VALLEY NATURE CENTER IN
ORDER TO PRESERVE THE AGRICULTURAL
HISTORY OF THE AREA. HE HOSTS SCHOOLS, CHURCH
GROUPS AND ANY OTHER INTERESTED PARTIES IN AN
EFFORT TO EDUCATE PEOPLE ABOUT THE LAND.

. . . . .

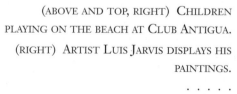

(ABOVE AND TOP, RIGHT) CHILDREN
PLAYING ON THE BEACH AT CLUB ANTIGUA.
(RIGHT) ARTIST LUIS JARVIS DISPLAYS HIS
PAINTINGS.

. . . . .

(OPPOSITE, TOP) TWILIGHT AT
FFRYES BAY BEACH.
(OPPOSITE, BOTTOM) SHELLS CAN BE FOUND
IN ABUNDANCE AT FFRYES BEACH.

(MAIN PHOTO) CLUB ANTIGUA BOASTS A VERITABLE
LOCAL MARKETPLACE WITHIN ITS PREMISES.
. . . . .

(ABOVE) SHOWING OFF A NEW HAIRDO—
MANY TOURISTS ARE TEMPTED TO HAVE THEIR HAIR
BRAIDED BY THE ANTIGUAN WOMEN WHO SET UP
"SHOP" ON THE BEACH.

THE PARISH OF
$\mathscr{S}$T. GEORGE

A slender strip running from the airport at the north end of the island down to the village of All Saints is the region known as the parish of St. George. V.C. Bird Airport is constructed on the same site that the first airport on Antigua—Coolidge Airfield—was built in 1941 by the U.S. Air Force. (Coolidge, by the way, does not refer to the U.S. president of the same name, but to a U.S. Army Air Corps hero who was killed in France during World War I.)

Off the northern tip of St. George are two islands: Maiden Island is populated only by herons, sandpipers and snails, whereas Long Island contains an exclusive resort, some vacation homes and an exquisite anchorage for yachts off the beach in Jumby Bay.

There are lovely views across Parham Sound to Long Island, Maiden Island and Crabbs Peninsula from the road that passes around the airport. Where the road divides on the south side of the airport, the left-hand fork leads to St. George's Church on Fitches Creek Bay, originally built in 1687.

The area known as Sea View Farm is renowned for its potteries. The potters, all women, make plant pots and coal pots (cooking pots fueled by charcoal). The natural Antiguan clay is fired in open pits behind the potters' houses and all the pottery is a reddish color. Nearby in Potter's Village one can find woodcarvers and other artisans.

(PAGE 76 AND RIGHT) THE LAST REMAINING GENUINE ANTIGUAN POTTERY AT SEA VIEW FARM. CONTINUING IN THE TRADITION OF THEIR MOTHERS AND GRANDMOTHERS, A SMALL NUMBER OF WOMEN GATHER CLAY INDIGENOUS TO ANTIGUA AND CREATE FUNCTIONAL "COAL POTS" FOR COOKING. THEY DO NOT USE ELECTRIC KILNS; INSTEAD, THEY FIRE THEIR POTS IN A LARGE PIT USING WOOD.

. . . . .

(BELOW) A COLORFUL HOUSE PAINTED IN RASTAFARIAN COLORS.

(PHOTOS PG. 76, 77 TOP, 78 JENNIFER MERANTO)

(ABOVE AND BELOW) SEVERAL
ARTISANS AND CRAFTSPEOPLE
HAVE SET UP SHOP IN POTTER'S
VILLAGE. CARL HENRY CREATES
WOOD SCULPTURE FROM
LOCALLY-GROWN TREES.
. . . . .

(ABOVE) PART OF THE WEST INDIAN MUSICAL HERITAGE AND CULTURE,
STEEL DRUMS ARE PREVALENT THROUGHOUT ANTIGUA AND THE CARIBBEAN.
THEIR DISTINCTIVE SOUND CAN BE HEARD AT MANY EVENTS.

· · · · ·

(OPPOSITE, IN SEQUENCE)
VINCENT FREELAND, WORLD-RENOWNED STEEL DRUM MAKER FROM PIGGOT'S VILLAGE,
DEMONSTRATES THE PROCESS OF MAKING A TENOR DRUM. HE FIRST SHAPES THE TOP OF THE DRUM BY
POUNDING IT WITH A HEAVY IRON MALLET. HE MEASURES THE DEPTH OF THE CURVE SIMPLY BY HOLDING
A STRAIGHT STICK ACROSS THE TOP OF THE BARREL AND MEASURING DOWN TO THE POUNDED SURFACE
TO CHECK THE DEPTH. IT IS IMPORTANT THAT THE METAL BE SHAPED EVENLY IN ORDER TO PRODUCE
A CLEAR AND ACCURATE TONE. HE THEN USES ANOTHER TOOL WITH NAIL GUIDES TO SCRIBE A LINE
AROUND THE EXTERNAL SURFACE OF THE BARREL INDICATING THE DEPTH TO WHICH HE WILL CUT THE
BARREL. EACH NAIL INDICATES THE DEPTH FOR A PARTICULAR TYPE OF DRUM—TENOR OR BASS, FOR
EXAMPLE. NEXT, HE CUTS THE DRUM WITH A COLD CHISEL AND A HAMMER. AFTER IT IS CUT, HE FOLDS
BACK THE SHARP EDGES TO MAKE A SMOOTH AND FINISHED EDGE. SOME STEEL DRUMS WILL EVENTUALLY
BE CHROME PLATED, DEPENDING ON THE FINANCIAL RESOURCES OF THE PARTICULAR BAND.

THE PARISH OF
St. PETER

The 17th century village of Parham in the parish of St. Peter is purported to have been the second most important port in Antigua after St. John's. Today Parham, with its historic buildings still in their original state, is just a sleepy village—a reminder of Antigua of yesterday. St. Peter's Anglican Church, octagonal in shape, is the most exceptional landmark—an ode to British Colonial days.

On the eastern side of Parham Bay is Crabbs Marina. Surrounded by factories and power lines, it is not the most aesthetic dockage, but it is a working boatyard and a good hurricane hole. Off Crabbs Peninsula is Great Bird Island, and two tiny spits of land, Redhead and Rabbit Islands, each veritable wildlife sancturies filled with nesting birds. Guiana Island, named after the first British settlers who fled Dutch Guiana (Surinam) in 1667 after the Treaty of Breda left that country in Dutch hands, is another small island of note. Originally a sugar plantation, it was turned into a park between the two World Wars. A pontoon with limited access connects it to the mainland.

Inland is Parham Hill Estates, and between the villages of Pares and Glanvilles are the ruins of Betty's Hope, one of the largest of the original sugar plantations. Two windmill towers are currently being restored. Also of note, but not necessarily a tourist attraction, is Potworks Dam, a reservoir created in the late 1960s. It is fed by streams that contribute to a significant body of water in the rainy season, but remains dry other times of the year. In any case, most water in Antigua is now made pure through the wonders of desalinization.

(PAGE 82) TYPICAL VILLAGE HOUSE.

· · · · ·

(ABOVE) WAITING FOR THE SHOPKEEPER. CARIBBEAN-STYLE WOODEN HOUSES
TRADITIONALLY USE SHUTTERS FOR WINDOWS AND DOORS.

(ABOVE) THE WATER TANK IN PARHAM HAS BEEN COLORFULLY ILLUMINATED
WITH A PAINTED MURAL.

. . . . .

(ABOVE) PARHAM VILLAGE WAS ONE OF THE
ORIGINAL SETTLEMENTS OF THE 17TH CENTURY.
(RIGHT) TWO YOUNG GIRLS FROM PARHAM
VILLAGE.
· · · · ·
(OPPOSITE) PARHAM ESTATE.

(OPPOSITE) THE CEMETERY IN FRONT OF ST. PETER'S CHURCH.

· · · · ·

(ABOVE) ALTHOUGH OTHER CHURCHES HAVE OCCUPIED THIS SITE, ST. PETER'S
CHURCH HAS STOOD SINCE THE EARLY 1840S. BUILT BY REV. FRANCIS BELL GRANT,
IT HAS AN UNUSUAL OCTAGONAL SHAPE. IN 1984, THE INTERIOR STUCCO
PLASTER WAS REMOVED TO SHOW THE ORIGINAL STONE.

(MAIN PHOTO) FOUNDED AROUND 1650,
BETTY'S HOPE WAS ANTIGUA'S FIRST SUGAR
PLANTATION. THE RESTORED MILL DATES BACK TO
1737. WHEN IT WAS OPERATIONAL, IT COULD
GRIND ABOUT 200 TONS OF CANE, PRODUCING 5,500
GALLONS OF SYRUP A WEEK.

· · · · ·

(BELOW) BETTY'S HOPE IS NOW A SHADY
REFUGE FOR A HERD OF GOATS.

THE PARISH OF
St. PHILIP

The parish of St. Philip covers the eastern end of Antigua and includes Green Island, which is the easternmost tip. A pleasant sojourn around this parish might take you from one of the main roads out of St. John's past the turn-off to Newfield, and on to the village of St. Philips. This sleepy little place—which takes its name from an Anglican church built there around 1690—has some adjacent bluffs that offer superb views of Willoughby Bay and the landmass of Chalky Hill and Savanna Estates. Following this road southeast to where it ends in a footpath will lead you to Half Moon Bay, one of the most beautiful beaches on the Atlantic side of the island. On the north side of Half Moon Bay is the private and exclusive Mill Reef Club. Conceived in 1948, it consists of a clubhouse, a variety of elegant villas and a nine-hole golf course. The club's property stretches over 1,300 acres that extend all the way to the south side of Nonsuch Bay, including all the small islands offshore.

When you leave this enclave you have to backtrack until you come to a fork in the road where instead of going back to St. Philips, you can travel north through Freetown. A pleasant surprise awaits you at the end of the road: Harmony Hall. This beautifully restored old estate house has been converted into a superb restaurant, inn and art gallery. The hospitable managers can organize a boat trip for you to Green Island, a favorite anchorage for yachtsmen at the gateway of Nonsuch Bay. Unspoiled by buildings, it abounds with bird life. You can picnic and swim on the beach, which, like all Antiguan beaches, is public; however, the rest of the island is under lease to the Mill Reef Club and is only accessible to members.

To explore the interesting sites at the northern end of the parish, you have

ANTIGUA

to get back on the main road and make a detour to the village of Seatons, a good spot for a magnificent panoramic view of Mercers Creek Bay. The main road passes through the village of Willikies and ends at Long Bay, a popular swimming beach.

Indian Town Point at the northeastern extremity of Antigua can be reached only by foot. The main attraction here is the natural limestone arch on the eastern side known as Devil's Bridge, named because the waves crashing over the "bridge" create some dramatic wild effects.

(PAGE 92) THE NORTHEASTERN POINT OF ANTIGUA IN AN AREA KNOWN AS INDIAN TOWN POINT. A PHENOMENON KNOWN AS DEVIL'S BRIDGE IS ACTUALLY A NATURAL LIMESTONE ARCH CARVED OUT BY CONSTANT WAVE ACTION FROM THE SEA.

. . . . .

(ABOVE) PICTURESQUE ST. PHILIP'S CHURCH

(ABOVE) VIEW SOUTH TOWARD FLAT POINT AND NONSUCH BAY FROM DEVIL'S BRIDGE.

. . . . .

(MAIN PHOTO) AERIAL VIEW OF GREAT DEEP BAY
AND MILL REEF FROM ABOVE YORK ISLAND.

. . . . .

(TOP RIGHT) MACUMBA BAR IS A
COLORFUL AND CHARMING WATERING HOLE
IN WILLIKIES.

(BOTTOM RIGHT) THOUGH THIS HOUSE IS TINY,
THE YARD IS TENDED WITH GREAT CARE.

(THIS PAGE) HARMONY HALL—AN OLD ESTATE HOUSE—HAS BEEN
BEAUTIFULLY RENOVATED TO CREATE AN ELEGANT GUEST HOUSE AND
RESTAURANT. A BAR IN THE OLD MILL AND AN ECLECTIC ART GALLERY
FEATURING CARIBBEAN AND OTHER ARTISTS ADDS TO ITS ATTRACTIVENESS.

. . . . .

(OPPOSITE) THE VAST EXTENT OF ANTIGUA'S CORAL REEFS CAN CLEARLY
BE SEEN IN THIS AERIAL VIEW LOOKING TOWARDS GREEN ISLAND.

THE ISLAND OF
BARBUDA

Barbuda is a low flat island, the highest point being only 125 feet above sea level. It is invisible from Antigua and in fact has no natural features which can be identified when entering from the sea. Surrounded by turquoise shoal water and coral reefs, this large landmass, half the size of Antigua, is a very quiet place. Approximately 1,600 inhabitants are concentrated around the village of Codrington, named after an old colonial plantation family who came to Antigua in the late 17th century. The family leased Barbuda from England to raise livestock and grow root crops for their estates in Antigua. Barbudans were originally imported as slaves to help the Codringtons maintain their holdings. Emancipation came in 1834, and in 1860 Barbuda was formally annexed to Antigua.

Change has come slowly to Barbuda. There is a small, rather shallow boat harbor, a couple of airstrips and a hotel or two. The beaches on Barbuda are superb—the ones on the south and west coasts are each several miles long and usually deserted. Visitors to Barbuda are limited to enjoying the wildlife—deer, birds and ducks—and activities such as shelling, beachcombing, fishing and snorkeling. The frigate bird colony is purported to be one of the largest in the world. Also of interest are several caves, the most interesting of which is Darby Sink Hole, a few miles northeast of Codrington. Historical sites are the River Fort built in the early part of the 19th century, probably used for observation, and the ruins of Highland House, where the Codrington family lived around 1750. All that is left is a cistern, some lower walls and the floors. Barbuda is definitely one of the few islands in the Caribbean where time has stood still.

(PAGE 100) ROOSTERS AND CHICKENS HAVE THE RUN OF THE ISLAND.

(OPPOSITE AND ABOVE) THE CHILDREN OF BARBUDA ARE NOT CAMERA-SHY.

· · · · ·

(TOP) THE BARBUDA COMMUNITY PRESCHOOL IS HOUSED IN AN
INTERESTING STONE BUILDING.

(ABOVE) ENTERING THE VILLAGE OF CODRINGTON IS LIKE STEPPING BACK IN TIME.
HOUSES ARE SIMPLE BUT RICH IN TEXTURE, AND LIFE IS SLOW AND LOW-KEY.

· · · · ·

(OPPOSITE) WOMAN DOING MORNING CHORES.

(OPPOSITE, TOP AND BOTTOM) SHUTTERS ON THE DOORS AND WINDOWS ARE COMMON.

· · · · ·

(TOP AND BOTTOM, LEFT) STONE WALLS SURROUNDED THE TOWN OF CODRINGTON IN
THE PAST. NOW THE TOWN HAS GROWN BEYOND THESE BOUNDARIES.

(BOTTOM, RIGHT) DECORATIVE FENCE.

(ABOVE) PINK SAND BEACH—MILES OF DESERTED BEACHES
SURROUND BARBUDA, MAKING THE ISLAND A BEACHCOMBER'S
PARADISE.

. . . . .

(BOTTOM, LEFT) THE BEACH AT RIVER FORT.

(BOTTOM, MIDDLE) LOW BAY BEACH IS A LONG NARROW
STRIP OF BEACH DIVIDING CODRINGTON LAGOON FROM THE
OCEAN. IT WAS FORMED DURING HURRICANE LUIS WHICH HIT
THE ISLAND IN 1995.

(BOTTOM, RIGHT) FROM A DISTANCE, AREAS OF THE BEACHES
GLISTEN WITH A ROSY GLOW; UPON CLOSER INSPECTION,
THESE BEACHES ARE MADE UP OF TINY PINK SHELLS.

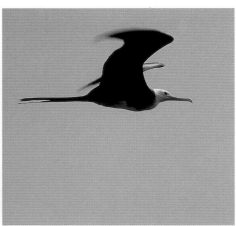

(ABOVE) THE FRIGATE BIRD NESTING COLONY, LOCATED ON THE NORTH END OF
CODRINGTON LAGOON, IS THE LARGEST NESTING COLONY OF THE MAGNIFICENT BLACK FRIGATE
BIRDS IN THE WORLD. VISITORS ARE TAKEN FROM THE VILLAGE LANDING IN BOATS TO VIEW THE
BIRDS. WITH A WING SPAN UP TO EIGHT FEET, THEY CAN SOAR UP TO 22 MPH TO
AN ALTITUDE OF 2,000 FEET. THE BIRDS ARE APPROACHABLE AND DO NOT APPEAR TO MIND
HAVING THEIR PICTURE TAKEN.

· · · · ·

(ABOVE) THE IMPRESSIVE RIVER FORT THAT INCLUDES THE 56-FOOT MARTELLO TOWER, ONE OF THE HIGHEST POINTS IN BARBUDA. SITUATED THREE MILES SOUTH OF CODRINGTON, IT WAS ORIGINALLY BUILT TO DEFEND THE MAIN ANCHORAGE AND TO BE USED AS A LOOKOUT FOR FOREIGN OR DISTRESSED SHIPS. BARBUDANS CLAIM THE TOWER HAS BEEN THERE SINCE THE LATE 17TH CENTURY; HOWEVER, ACCORDING TO SOME CODRINGTON PAPERS, IT IS MORE LIKELY THAT IT WAS BUILT MUCH LATER. THE FORT IS CURRENTLY BEING RESTORED.

. . . . .

(RIGHT) SEAGRAPE TREES HELP PRESERVE THE BEACHES.

(ABOVE) THE HIGHLANDS ARE DOTTED WITH NUMEROUS CAVES AND SINK HOLES, WHICH ARE
DEPRESSION IN THE GROUND WITH CLIFF-LIKE SIDES.

. . . . .

(OPPOSITE, TOP AND BOTTOM LEFT) THE HIGHLANDS AREA OF BARBUDA IS RUGGEDLY BEAUTIFUL.

(OPPOSITE, BOTTOM RIGHT) THE RUINS OF HIGHLAND HOUSE, THE CODRINGTON'S RESIDENTIAL COMPLEX,
CONSISTS OF THE HOUSE, STABLES, WATER CISTERN AND A COUPLE OF HUNDRED FEET OF AQUEDUCT. THERE
IS NO PROOF OF THE EXACT DATE OF CONSTRUCTION, BUT CERAMIC SHARDS INDICATE OCCUPANCY FROM
AROUND 1730 UNTIL THE EARLY 1800S. ACCORDING TO A NAUTICAL HANDBOOK WRITTEN IN 1836, THE SITE,
THOUGH IN RUINS, WAS CLEARLY USED AT LEAST FOR NAVIGATIONAL PURPOSES. DESMOND NICHOLSON
INDICATES THE MEDIAN DATE TO BE AROUND 1768 IN HIS BOOK, *HERITAGE LANDMARKS* .
THE BARBUDANS' NAME FOR THIS PLACE IS "WILLYBOB."

THE TRADITION OF
ℐACHTING

Situated midway in the Leeward chain of islands in the Lesser Antilles, Antigua's history and present are intertwined with the sea and boats. With all its bays and inlets and ever-increasing marinas and yachting facilities, Antigua is extremely popular with cruising yachts. Commodore V.E.B. Nicholson sailed his old schooner *Mollyhawk* into a deserted English Harbour with his wife, brother, and sons, Rodney and Desmond, in 1948. They established a base at Nelson's Dockyard and ever since the family has been extremely influential in developing Antigua as a yachting hub. The annual Nicholson Charter Show, now in its 37th year (1998), is regarded as *the* international charter show, rivaling the famous St. Remo show in the Mediterranean. Between 150-200 world-class motoryachts and sailboats line the docks in English and Falmouth Harbours.

The other major yachting events are the Sportfishing Tournament, the world-famous Antigua Sailing Week, and the Classic Yacht Regatta, held just prior to Sailing Week. Antigua Sailing Week had its inception in 1968. Every year it has become larger and larger. Yachts from at least 20 countries race in eight different classes under International Yacht Racing Rules. There are five races spread over seven days, preceded by two passage races. Serious partying certainly does go on, but the racing remains quite competitive.

The Classic Week, which evolved from Sailing Week, was organized primarily for old wooden boats; however, not all entries are old and not all are wooden. There is a "Spirit of Tradition" class for yachts based on classic designs, but executed with new technologies.

All in all, Antigua is a yachting paradise!

(PAGE 114) A GAFF-RIGGED KETCH AND HER LITTLE SISTER.

(PAGES 116-117) IN 1988 A GROUP OF CLASSIC YACHT SKIPPERS DECIDED IT
WOULD BE FUN TO REVIVE THE ORIGINAL CONCEPT OF "RACE WEEK." EIGHT VINTAGE
YACHTS RACED DOWN TO GUADELOUPE AND BACK, WHICH WAS THE BIRTH OF THE
CLASSIC YACHT REGATTA. NOW OLD AND NEW CLASSICS FROM ALL OVER THE WORLD
MAKE THIS EVENT PART OF THEIR CRUISING SCHEDULE. IN 1998 ONE OF THE
TALL SHIPS PARTICIPATED.

· · · · ·

(PAGES 118-119) DURING ANTIGUA SAILING WEEK
THE COURSES OF BETWEEN 16 AND 28 MILES
ARE DESIGNED TO CHALLENGE THE VARIOUS
POINTS OF SAIL AS WELL AS TACKING TECHNIQUES.
THE DOWNWIND SPINNAKER RUN IS ALWAYS A
SIGHT TO BEHOLD.

(PHOTOS THESE TWO PAGES BY ROGER LEAN-VERCOE)

· · · · ·

(TOP) "LAY DAY" DURING SAILING WEEK
IS A DAY OF PARTYING, PRIZES, MUSIC,
GAMES AND FRIVOLITIES.

. . . . .

(BOTTOM AND OPPOSITE) SAILING WEEK HAS
TURNED INTO ONE OF THE FOREMOST REGATTAS
IN THE WORLD, BRINGING THOUSANDS OF
ENTHUSIASTS, SPECTATORS, PRESS, PHOTOGRAPHERS
AND CREWS FOR THE TRADITIONAL SEASON-END
PARTY, BEFORE THE YACHTS DISPERSE OFF TO THE FAR
CORNERS OF THE WORLD FOR THE SUMMER.

(PHOTOS THESE TWO PAGES BY ROGER LEAN-VERCOE)

ACKNOWLEDGMENTS

In creating this book, we have been very fortunate to have had the vision, assistance and kindness from many people. Christian Chalmin of Boat International Publications had the idea for the book, and encouraged us to work on it sooner rather than later. Hon. Dr. Rodney Williams, Minister of Tourism, Culture, and Environment, along with Irma Tomlinson, offered additional encouragement and assisted with valuable logistics. Desmond Nicholson, the originator of the Dockyard Museum, kindly availed us of his wisdom on historical events, as well as providing us with priceless old photos from his library. His assistant Penny Thoms and her colleagues at the National Park Authority lent us a hand proofing our text—all in the face of great adversity as our press deadline was exquisitely timed with Hurricane Georges and the subsequent floods and power outages. Kenny Coombs provided us with his knowledge and expertise on Sailing and Classic Week. Caribbean Helicopters, Catamaran Hotel, Club Antigua, Halcyon Heights, Sandpiper Reef Resort and Siboney Beach Club were helpful and generous. We are extremely appreciative of the photographers who helped us fill in some of the holes in our repertoire: Alexis Andrews, Jennifer Moranto, and Roger Lean-Vercoe. And we have great respect for, and are exceedingly grateful to, our colleagues in Vermont who helped us pull this book together: Bonnie Atwater, designer par excellence; Deborah Wolfe, our efficient office manager; and Janet Hubbard-Brown, our diligent copy editor. Also, special mention to Dana's husband B'fer Roth who carried camera bags and took notes on one of her more significant forays to Antigua and Barbuda. We would also like to thank Flip for being our eternal Antigua connection, Gay Gemmill for distributing our book, and lastly we would like to thank Hugh Piggot and all of the wonderful people of the islands who showed us an Antigua and Barbuda we never knew.